T0056723

THE LITTLE GREEN BOOK OF
TENNIS WISDOM

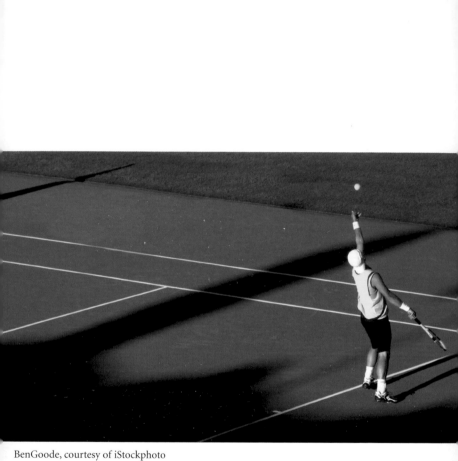
BenGoode, courtesy of iStockphoto

THE LITTLE GREEN BOOK OF
TENNIS WISDOM

Edited by
Julie Ganz

Skyhorse Publishing

Skyhorse Publishing books may be purchased in bulk at special discounts for sales promotion, corporate gifts, fund-raising, or educational purposes. Special editions can also be created to specifications. For details, contact the Special Sales Department, Skyhorse Publishing, 307 West 36th Street, 11th Floor, New York, NY 10018 or info@skyhorsepublishing.com.

Skyhorse® and Skyhorse Publishing® are registered trademarks of Skyhorse Publishing, Inc.®, a Delaware corporation.

Visit our website at www.skyhorsepublishing.com.

10 9 8 7 6 5 4 3 2 1

Library of Congress Cataloging-in-Publication Data is available on file.

Photo on pages iv-vii ©JOFoster, courtesy of iStockphoto

Cover design by Tom Lau
Cover photo credit Shutterstock

ISBN: 978-1-5107-0628-6
Ebook ISBN: 978-1-5107-0629-3

Printed in China

To my sister, who will always be my partner of choice on the tennis court.

Acknowledgments

To all of those tennis players, coaches, and gurus whose words inspired me, thank you.

To my husband, who dealt with my quote-finding quest for months on end, thank you for your patience.

And to my parents, without whom I would never have developed a passion for this sport for life, an extra special thank you!

Contents

	Introduction	ix
Part One	History and Evolution of the Game	1
Part Two	Strategy and More Musings from the Wise	37
Part Three	Grand Slams	94
Part Four	Davis Cup	114
Part Five	More Reflections and Insight from the Pros	120
Part Six	Apparel	194
Part Seven	Doubles	199
Part Eight	A Shout-out to Table Tennis (Also Known as Ping-Pong)	205
	References	208
	Index	211

INTRODUCTION

I've experienced every emotion when it comes to tennis, which is one of the reasons I love the game so much. No, it's not always easy on the body, nor is it always fair on the mind. The quotes in this book from legendary tennis writers and players like Bud Collins, Steve Tignor, Jon Wertheim, John McEnroe, Arthur Ashe, Roger Federer, Monica Seles, Billie Jean King, and this year's *Sports Illustrated* Sportsperson of the Year, Serena Williams, prove just that. History has not always been easy on the tennis players (or the fans, for that matter), but in many other ways, it has been incredibly rewarding and magical, proving its reputation as a game for life.

When I think back on my experience of playing tennis as a youth, mostly I feel happy, reflecting on a strong backhand down the line or a sharp volley at the net that sends my opponent flailing and my doubles partner over to "clink" her racket against mine. Or I recall my grandparents watching my sister and me battling it out under the Florida sun and making us feel like we were capable of a Williams sisters feat—the ultimate compliment, of course. But reflections of life on the tennis court bring up some intense feelings of frustration as well, over the forehand that doesn't have enough topspin or the serve that just can't seem to catch enough speed.

Tennis is also one of those games that gets under your skin. There's a reason that "love" is a big part of the sport. Regrettably, life in the big city does not offer as many opportunities to play tennis, but I feel fortunate to have developed a passion for the game at a young age, an adoration that will never cease, regardless of how often I make it out onto a court these days.

A few months ago, my husband and I visited the museum at Wimbledon. It was a fairly long walk from the tube station to the tennis complex, and at certain points I wondered if we'd made a wrong turn. But then suddenly, I heard a familiar "pop," and there in front of us was one of the side courts. It was almost odd, the sense of calm that immediately engulfed me upon our arrival there. The sense of excitement and feeling that I was somewhere special and historic was irreplaceable.

I hope the quotes that follow take you through a wide range of emotions. I hope they make you laugh, cry, think, or learn something. I hope they make you feel like you're on Centre Court, even if you're miles away.

—Julie Ganz
Winter 2015

PART ONE

History and Evolution
of the Game

The name first applied to court tennis and later to lawn
tennis is elusive and mysterious . . . The word that began as
tenes and ended as *tennis* has passed through twenty-four
transformations, four variations of five letters, twelve of six
letters, seven of seven letters, and one of eight letters.
—MALCOLM D. WHITMAN,
Tennis: Origins and Mysteries

• • •

Unlike sports such as baseball and golf that revere their champions of the past, tennis increasingly tries to distance itself from them.

—RON COBB

• • •

It is not only the sum of ball games. It is the absolute in games. No one, it is probable, has yet sounded the depths of court tennis, and players of the greatest genius cannot master its fine potentialities.

—*LONDON SPECTATOR* (1912)

• • •

[Major Walter Wingfield] popularized this game enormously.
He was absolutely terrific at marketing and he sent his
game all over the world.

— HONOR GODFREY

•   •   •

By all accounts, even allowing for a degree of sycophantic
flattery, [Henry VIII] was a world-class [tennis] player.

—ALISON WEIR,
Henry VIII: The King and His Court

•   •   •

Before the Open era, tennis was, as Bud Collins once called it, the "secret sport," hidden away from America's great unwashed behind ivy-covered walls.

—STEVE TIGNOR

• • •

The arrival of Open tennis forty years ago indisputably helped turn tennis players into household names. It brought the sport's professionals—its biggest stars, its largest personalities—into the game.

—USTA,
The Open Book

• • •

In those heady days, so influenced by the egalitarian revolution of the 1960s, grass was not a substance on which you played tennis but an illicit weed that you smoked.

—PETER BODO,
The Courts of Babylon

• • •

It's an abnormal world I live in. It's like I'm floating down the middle. I'm never quite sure where I am. It does bother me that I'm in this predicament, but I don't dwell on it, because I know it will resolve itself.

—ARTHUR ASHE

• • •

Bogaerts, Rob/Anefo, via Wikimedia Commons

Anyone who wouldn't watch Arthur Ashe play tennis wouldn't watch Picasso paint, Hemingway write, a diamond cut, Astaire dance, or Gielgud act. Nobody calls him "Art," but he is.

—JIM MURRAY

As he turned back the field at the US Open past week, Arthur Ashe seemed a spectator to his own success.

—DAVID WOLF

Like the Babe or [boxer Jack] Dempsey, [Ashe] found a sport chained in the dungeon and subsisting on bread and water. Everybody was playing tennis but no one was watching it.

—JIM MURRAY

• • •

I'd much rather people knew me as a good tennis player than as an aboriginal who happens to play good tennis. Of course I'm proud of my race, but I don't want to be thinking about it all the time.

—EVONNE GOOLAGONG

• • •

Arthur [Ashe] and Billie Jean [King] tore down foundations.
They did this to enable people to have a chance to survive in life.
Without people like them, tennis wouldn't be where it is today.
—NICK BOLLETTIERI,
Bollettieri: Changing the Game

• • •

What the women got out of when I beat [Bobby] Riggs was
self-confidence and higher self-esteem. For the first time
they were asking for a raise, for instance.
—BILLIE JEAN KING

• • •

Billie Jean King is a global treasure.
—HOLLY HUNTER,
Pressure Is a Privilege (Preface)

• • •

That match will haunt me forever.
—MARGARET COURT,
Court on Court (on the Battle of the Sexes against Bobby Riggs)

• • •

AP Photo/Harry Harris

I did not want anything to set back the struggle that I and so many other women were enduring, and I wondered what would happen if I—or any other woman—lost to Bobby [Riggs].

—BILLIE JEAN KING,
Pressure Is a Privilege

• • •

I told the committee yesterday I would play only on center court. I'm the defending champion, and I don't see why I can't play in center court instead of another women's singles match.

—PATRICIA CANNING TODD

• • •

I've always been regarded as an upstart who didn't really belong in exalted company.
—FRED PERRY,
Fred Perry, An Autobiography

• • •

AP Photo

Tennis belongs to the individualistic past—a hero, or at most a pair of friends or lovers—against the world.

—JACQUES BARZUN

• • •

Instead of Fred J. Perry the champ I felt like J. Fred Muggs the chimp. The Perry balloon was certainly deflated.

— FRED PERRY,
after winning his first title

• • •

[Andy] Murray has definitely nailed the title of the greatest British player of all time. Fred Perry was fantastic, but this era throws up some very different challenges.

—GREG RUSEDSKI

• • •

[Bill] Tilden is more of an artist than nine-tenths of the artists
I know. It is the beauty of the game that Tilden loves.
It is the chase always, rather than the quarry.
—FRANKLIN ADAMS

• • •

If American tennis ever had a golden boy, it was the
handsome, flaxen-haired [Joe] Hunt, who won the US singles
championship a half century ago at Forest Hills in the last
match of his life.
—BUD COLLINS

• • •

If Althea Gibson represents a challenge to the present crop of players, then it's only fair that they meet this challenge on the courts.
——ALICE MARBLE

• • •

[Bill] Tilden was a central figure in the evolution of his sport, and until he lost to [Henri] Cochet there was no better big-match player.
——STEVE FLINK,
The Greatest Tennis Matches of All Time

• • •

I was playing a little faster in my day and you didn't have quite as much time to set up to hit the two-hander, so you'd either have to let go or stretch out and not be able to hit it as well, so the two-handers are easier to hit [now] not because players are moving so well, they're getting the ball and are able to get both hands on the racket when they hit it.

—STAN SMITH

• • •

[Bjorn] Borg and [John] McEnroe—righty vs. lefty, defender vs. attacker, ice vs. fire, machine vs. mad genius, civilization vs. its discontents—was a rivalry made in tennis heaven.

—STEVE TIGNOR

• • •

When it comes to conjuring up memories of what made tennis
so inviting to people who grew up in the 1960s, 1970s,
and 1980s, it's the classic clashes of the New Yorker
[McEnroe] and the Swede [Borg] that first come to mind.

—MATTHEW CRONIN,

Epic

• • •

Starting with Björn Borg, tennis players became more than just
sports stars. Back then, even rock musicians aspired to be touring
tennis pros. (Of course, *we* all aspired to be rock musicians.)

—JOHN MCENROE,

Serious

• • •

Antonio García from Madrid, Spain, via Wikimedia Commons

[Björn Borg] was bigger than the game. He was like
Elvis or Liz Taylor or somebody.
——ARTHUR ASHE

• • •

Connors was then the finest tennis player in the world.
In fact, the match was supposed to be a slaughter, and I was
to be the sacrificial lamb.
——ARTHUR ASHE,
in *Days of Grace*, with Arnold Rampersad

• • •

Playing for himself, for his country, for posterity, he was invincible. [Bill] Tilden simply was tennis in the public mind.
——FRANK DEFORD,
Big Bill Tilden

• • •

Rod [Laver] does his job extremely competently and thoroughly. No show, no emotion. Like a good plumber. A plumber doesn't put on a show down there alone in the basement, does he? On the court Rod is totally oblivious to his surroundings.
——LEMEAU WATT

• • •

A few seconds after Roche's final forehand sailed out,
Laver found himself in mid-air. He leapt across the net,
and into tennis history.
—STEVE TIGNOR,
on Rod Laver's 1969 Grand Slam

• • •

It was a thrill to come off the court knowing I had won all four
majors in one year. But I never felt like I was the best, never felt
that way. I just happened to have a good year.
—ROD LAVER

• • •

In the early 1970s, the garish "optic yellow" of the modern tennis ball was the color of change, and Mike Davies, who helped transform tennis from a country club pastime to a billion-dollar sports enterprise, embraced it.

——STEVE CHAWKINS

• • •

The most shocking events in my thirty-five years–plus of playing tennis was the day Vitas Gerulaitis died; the day it came out that Arthur Ashe was HIV positive and the day he died; and the day Monica [Seles] was stabbed.

——PAM SHRIVER

• • •

History and Evolution of the Game

We in the US have such a sophisticated, cluttered, and popular sports marketplace. Face it: just about every little kid rapidly absorbs the language of football, baseball, and basketball. But tennis is rather arcane, a subculture. More and more I think the American tennis boom of the '70s was a freaky occurrence.

—JOEL DRUCKER

• • •

They weren't cheering Martina the Complainer, or Martina the Czech, Martina the Loser, Martina the Bisexual Defector. They were cheering me. I had never felt anything like it in my life. Acceptance, respect, maybe even love.

—MARTINA NAVRATILOVA

• • •

Much like the Fab Five changed basketball, Andre Agassi changed tennis. His rock and roll persona amped up the quiet game drawing the attention of the MTV generation and Hollywood elite.

—IAN STONEBROOK

• • •

If American tennis's Golden Age was in the 1990s, Australia's in the '60s, and Spain's around [2012], France had the decade extending five years before and after 1930.

—REEVES WIEDEMAN

• • •

For US tennis [Lindsay Davenport] was the American girl, the girl next door and always very humble. For me, she has been an absolute paragon and I hope there's another Lindsay Davenport out there coming along because she's done a tremendous amount for American tennis and women's tennis.

—JANE BROWN GRIMES

• • •

The tennis is twice as good [today], the points they play . . .
You've got to be more of an athlete probably today. We were
pretty darn good—fit and ready to play—but today's level
is different. Those ground strokes are ever so much faster,
coming back at you at a pretty good speed. Footwork-wise,
you've got to be ready to hit that next shot. It's a tough time.

—ROD LAVER

• • •

Yankees and Red Sox, Ali and Frazier, Borg and McEnroe. These
are great rivalries, and rivalries make each side better.

—WALTER IOOSS

• • •

A choke is throwing a wild pitch in Game 7 of the World Series or calling a timeout in the NCAA championships when you don't have any. Serena's loss was the culmination of nine months of building pressure that finally reared its paralyzing head.

—CHRIS CHASE,
on the quest for a Serena Slam

• • •

I look up to her so much. Winning or in defeat. I would trade 10 of my good days for one bad day of Serena's.

—LOLO JONES,
track and field and bobsled athlete

• • •

That's what she's done for sixteen years now. We can't penalize
Serena because she's been winning everything for so long.
Someone shouldn't be punished because
we've grown to expect it from them.

—ANDY RODDICK

• • •

Tatiana, via Wikimedia Commons

Serena Williams is the greatest player I've ever seen. That doesn't change. Sometimes, the best player doesn't win.
—MIKE GREENBERG

• • •

It's unbelievable. I'm in the final. It's like a dream. . . . It's the best moment of my life.
—ROBERTA VINCI

• • •

In the early days the chair umpires and line judges were nervous they were going to be shown up. Very consistently over the course of a season, the players are correct 30 percent of the time. That is 70 percent the umpire or line judge got it correct and proves they have done a pretty good job.

—LUKE AGGAS,
Director of Tennis, Hawk-Eye Innovations

• • •

The return has become a very important part of the game. Before, when the courts were extremely quick, it was a different game. Guys were holding serve a lot more than they are now. That was a bit because of the surface. I just think that the return is maybe more important than the serve now because of the [slower] surface.

—ANDY MURRAY

• • •

BenGoode, courtesy of iStockphoto

Like moderate Republicans and anything Netscape, the classic
serve-and-volley style is all but extinct, a victim of shifting mores,
disruptive technology, and competitive obsolescence.

—PATRICK HRUBY

• • •

I'm not a big fan of [bad] tennis behavior. I like Federer because
he resembles the class I remember as being dominant. We didn't
have players grunting, yelling, carrying on. There was dignity in
the stands, on court. Now it's like hockey. It's out of control.

—ROBERT REDFORD

• • •

[Stan] Wawrinka's late rise to world-class player is, however, indicative of a broader trend in men's tennis: A sport that once favored fresh-faced youngsters has become the dominion of more seasoned statesmen.
—KEVIN CRAFT (JUNE 2015)

• • •

PART TWO

Strategy and More Musings from the Wise

Computers can do nothing without the software to tell them what to do. By the same token, tennis strokes are equally useless without proper strategies to give them direction.

—ALLEN FOX,
Think to Win

• • •

Whoever said "It's not whether you win or lose that counts"
probably lost.
——MARTINA NAVRATILOVA

• • •

It's the smallest thing in tennis that can make a change
in the biggest way.
——VICTORIA AZARENKA

• • •

Anything can happen in tennis.
—PATRICK MOURATOGLOU

• • •

Some people say I have attitude—maybe I do . . . but I think
you have to. You have to believe in yourself when no one
else does—that makes you a winner right there.
—VENUS WILLIAMS

• • •

si.robi, via Wikimedia Commons

You've got to have that hate. I hate Venus when I'm playing her.
——SERENA WILLIAMS

• • •

[Serena Williams] told me that I have to teach her the drop shots.
I said, "Well, you have to teach me the rest."
——TIMEA BACSINSZKY

• • •

You neutralize the opponent and you sort of wear him down.
Eventually someone is going to miss.
—ROGER FEDERER

• • •

Getting to 1,000 wins is more difficult than it seems. It's really
rare. But I looked at it as a by-product of winning so many
matches and being consistent for that long.
—IVAN LENDL

• • •

Jiblet, courtesy of iStockphoto

You knew every tear, every illness, every moment on court was true. You knew winning gave [Pete Sampras] a release he needed nearly as much as breathing.

—S. L. PRICE

• • •

Even when I was No. 1 in the world I was taking it one match at a time. . . . I think the most important thing in Slams is trying to find a way through the first week and then focus on starting fresh the second week if you can.

—LLEYTON HEWITT

• • •

If I don't practice the way I should, then I won't play the way I know I can.

—IVAN LENDL

• • •

If you don't practice, you don't deserve to win.

—ANDRE AGASSI

• • •

I play what I feel. I respond to the ball.
—MARTINA HINGIS

• • •

SteveCollender, courtesy of iStockphoto

I never look ahead in a Grand Slam. A lot of things can change.
—KIM CLIJSTERS

• • •

What is the single most important quality in a tennis champion?
I would have to say desire, staying in there and winning
matches when you are not playing that well.
—JOHN MCENROE

• • •

If I'm up a break in a set, I can just ride out my serve. That
doesn't necessarily mean that I'm tanking the return games, but
it gives me the opportunity to conserve energy for the service
game, knowing that I have that break in hand.
—JOHN ISNER

• • •

The objective, in a time of an overload of diversions and
challenged attention spans, should be variety: a chance for
all the strokes in this tough and technical game to
still have a legitimate place.

—CHRISTOPHER CLAREY

• • •

Once in a while you can do those things a little bit better, a little
bit differently and be more creative out there. I don't want to
see cookie-cutter players. I want to see creative players.

—MARTINA NAVRATILOVA

• • •

I can remember losing matches, and people would come up to
me and say, "Girl, do you know how many times you missed
that drop shot? If you hadn't done that, blah blah blah."
And I'd say, "Thank you." But I knew I had to do it.
That's what would win for me.

—DORIS HART

• • •

Like tennis, [in boxing] if you are prepared to sacrifice just a little
more than your opponent, it will give you an advantage. If you've
done the extra mile, you might have the better of him.

—ANDY MURRAY

• • •

Nobody in tennis is unbeatable.
——CHRIS CHASE

• • •

The mental side is an important part of the tennis puzzle. If you are able to master all areas of being a professional athlete, you can be successful.
——TOMÁŠ BERDYCH

• • •

Are tennis and acting alike? I don't know. They're both very mental games. They're both very heavy things to be a part of.

——MATTHEW PERRY

• • •

I used to be good at tennis . . . but when I'm not working, doing nothing is more appealing than a hobby.

——LISA KUDROW

• • •

I think conversation is a big thing in analyzing tennis
and situations in games.

——JIMMY CONNORS

• • •

Me, I want to let my racket do the talking.

——PETE SAMPRAS

• • •

Craig ONeal, via Wikimedia Commons

It is funny that balls are not spoken about, but they have a massive impact on a tournament and a player. Some find it very difficult [to adapt to changes from tournament to tournament]. The first thing we do when we get to the tournament is work out what tension [the racket] will be with that ball.
——DAVID TAYLOR

• • •

Matches are won and lost so many times in the locker room.
——LLEYTON HEWITT

• • •

Playing tennis is a job. It's good to have some friends, but you can only have a limited number. It's just not easy to be friends with a lot of the girls when you're going to be competing against them each week.

——EUGENIE BOUCHARD

• • •

Lleyton Hewitt's like electricity. He loves the team environment, and he's been a good mentor to young Australian players. He's left a great legacy and his records will stand for a long time.

——ANDY MURRAY

• • •

The past champions of every era always had a place to get to, a safe zone. Pete [Sampras's] backhand wasn't that strong. Andre [Agassi's] movement wasn't that strong. You go through every single player and they all had a slight weakness that you could attack. Lleyton [Hewitt] of that period, he did not.

—DARREN CAHILL

• • •

Playing professional tennis as a living, that was the best thing I knew and the best thing that I could do. So I wanted to keep at it as long as I was fit and healthy and basically enjoying the competition and winning a fair share of matches.

—KEN ROSEWALL

• • •

For 90 percent of the players, the two-hander [backhand]
offers more benefits.

—NICK BOLLETTIERI

• • •

[Stan Wawrinka] can wake up in the middle of the night
but still play an amazing backhand.

—MAGNUS NORMAN (COACH)

• • •

simonkr, courtesy of iStockphoto

If you have a big serve, a serve-and-volley tactic every once in a while has to be a good thing.

——PETER FLEMING

• • •

The serve-and-volley game is almost extinct, so if guys aren't at net, they're not hitting overheads. The less you hit, the worse the [overhead] shot becomes.

——MIKE BRYAN

• • •

Getting the first serve in is the key to winning for a serve-and-volleyer. It's something you're constantly thinking about. If you have to hit a second serve, you'll face either tough returns to volley or you'll be forced to stay back.

——STAN SMITH

• • •

ilbusca, courtesy of iStockphoto

When young athletes face the pressure at seventeen or
eighteen years old of ITF junior rankings and earning
college scholarships, they often opt for the route that
will have them winning the most matches at a young
age—which, of course, is the power game.

—NICK BOLLETTIERI

• • •

The first player that breaks down will most likely lose in the
pressure moments. And I was that player for some time, of
course, but I managed to learn and believe I can improve.
—NOVAK DJOKOVIC

• • •

Among my favorite features of the sport is that *tennis is ageless.*
More than a pastime, tennis is a lifetime activity.
—ANNA CLARK

• • •

A good punch in the nose—that's the volley. A short, stiff
jab with almost no backswing. You're blocking
the ball, not stroking it.

—ROD LAVER,
The Education of a Tennis Player

• • •

Sure, on a given day I could beat him. But it would have to
be a day he had food poisoning.

—MEL PURCELL,
on Ivan Lendl

• • •

I like Asian food. I like sushi. I've never met a tennis player
that hates sushi. It's weird. It's really weird.
——SERENA WILLIAMS

• • •

There had been so much tension and emotion out there for so
long that the end was just such a release. I was like: "It's over
at last, now I can go and eat!"
——JOHANNA KONTA

• • •

Losing is not my enemy . . . fear of losing is my enemy.
—RAFAEL NADAL

• • •

Talent takes you only so far. But the rest of it is you have to
teach it to yourself and learn it, get it right.
—ROGER FEDERER

• • •

Carine06 from UK, via Wikimedia Commons

I didn't feel like I was striking the ball quite the way
I would have liked—that's when you've got to grit
your teeth and hang in there.
—LLEYTON HEWITT

• • •

If, in a few months, I'm only number eight or number ten in the
world, I'll have to look at what off-the-court work I can do.
I will need to do something if I want to be number one.
—JOHN MCENROE

• • •

All the guys that are out there fighting each week to get to No. 1
are very hungry to get to No. 1.

—NOVAK DJOKOVIC

• • •

I think you need to work double as hard when you're up there.
If you're at the top of tennis, you're on tour thirty-plus weeks of
the year—and when you're doing that, everything revolves
around tennis. Every decision you make, tennis is at
the back of your mind.

—BARRY COWAN

• • •

It is a privilege having pressure, being a part of this beautiful sport. I am very grateful to have played tennis since I was four years old, when I began to dream of being World No. 1 and a multiple Grand Slam champion.

—NOVAK DJOKOVIC

• • •

Few sports have the global talent pool of tennis, so an ascent to the game's peak requires inordinate athleticism, ambition, mental fortitude, and luck.

—TOM PERROTTA

• • •

I needed to make mistakes to become the player I am today.
In a way I would do it again the same way, with just some
minor adjustments along the way.

—ROGER FEDERER

• • •

Everyone says that I'm so focused on the court and people ask me
why and how and [if] you're born with it or not. And to
be clear, I don't really know if you are. I think it's
something that you learn.

—MARIA SHARAPOVA

• • •

llanswart, courtesy of iStockphoto

I feel like as I started losing, I started getting more fans.
——PETE SAMPRAS

• • •

Tennis purists loved his skill, naturally, and they will
unhesitatingly declare Sampras's second serve, his running
forehand and his leaping overhead as treasures that
belong under museum glass.
——S. L. PRICE

• • •

In tennis, it is not the opponent you fear, it is the failure itself, knowing how near you were but just out of reach.

—ANDY MURRAY

• • •

Pressure grows simply with experience. When you're a kid, you don't feel it; you just hit the ball. When you get older, it means more.

—MARTINA NAVRATILOVA

• • •

At the end life has much more important things than win or lose a tennis match or a match in any sport. So when you get calm and you have the chance to think about all of this, sometimes you feel very stupid feeling this pressure, this nervous at the end for a tennis match. Not gonna change your life.

—RAFAEL NADAL

• • •

François GOGLINS, via Wikimedia Commons

In life, things don't always go the way you want, or in the direction you want, and tennis is the same, it's not special. So it's okay, because we can accept that sometimes we have good seasons and sometimes we have bad seasons. We have good tournaments and we have bad tournaments.

—TONI NADAL

• • •

"Nothing to lose" means I can go out there and try to play like I'm playing, without pressure, without nothing.

—ANGELIQUE KERBER

• • •

Tennis is an individual sport. But it is also a game you cannot play alone.
—DOUGLAS ROBSON

• • •

Henri Cochet can beat everybody when his shots are working and be beaten by everybody when they are not.
—RENÉ LACOSTE

• • •

Sure, the tennis nuts sound like they're repeating themselves,
all of the *awesome* and *epic* and *classic*. It's OK. Give us
a break. Not every event can match the interplanetary
thrill of the NFL draft. At least tennis fans are
arguing about actual tennis.

—JASON GAY

• • •

The fans are another reason why I play tennis! I play for
them all over the world.

—VICTORIA AZARENKA

• • •

Tennis opened my eyes to a lot of things. It gave me an opportunity to travel the world and meet some of the nicest people around, so what else could you ask for? It certainly beat milking cows back in Australia.

—ROY EMERSON

• • •

If, while learning tennis, you begin to learn how to trust in yourself, you have learned something far more valuable than how to hit a forceful backhand.

—W. TIMOTHY GALLWEY,
The Inner Game of Tennis

• • •

simonkr, courtesy of iStockphoto

I think the sport brings so many opportunities to women. It's brought me so many things in my life and my career. I don't regret any step I have taken. On the other hand, sometimes I wake up and think, "Well, I don't wish this on my kids!" But then when I'm playing the matches, I'm in front of thousands of people and the experience that the sport brings, I think, "Of course I want my kids to do this."

——MARIA SHARAPOVA

• • •

My game is always good when my movements are good, when I am able to have control of the point with my forehand, and always hitting good backhands. But the forehand need to be aggressive, need to create space with my forehand.

——RAFAEL NADAL

• • •

I didn't always have a great forehand, but if I was playing somebody with a great forehand, I knew how to mess them up.

——SHANNON ELIZABETH

• • •

Consistency is a mental weapon.

——NICK BOLLETTIERI

• • •

The foundation of a winning tennis player is not power and aggression but consistency and control.
—GREG MORAN,
Tennis Beyond Big Shots

• • •

The willingness of a player to return to the center of the court, when the opponent is in control of the point (unless they anticipate where the opponent will hit next and thus forego moving to the center), is a barometer of the player's confidence, fitness and interest in that game.
—DEVIL IN A NEW DRESS (BLEACHERREPORT.COM WRITER)

• • •

I've always considered myself the best and the top. I never
considered that I was out of it.
——SERENA WILLIAMS

• • •

I don't have the big serve where I can hit 35 aces in a match, but I
do have a way to fight myself into every match. To never give up
and fight till the last point.
——KEI NISHIKORI

• • •

A great tennis career is something that a fifteen-year-old normally doesn't have. I hope my example helps other teens believe they can accomplish things they never thought possible.

—MARIA SHARAPOVA

• • •

You have to think, but if you think too much—I have so many ideas. In your mind it's like, "Okay, I go down the line, then crosscourt, maybe drop shot." But you have just one second, or even not one second, it just has to be automatic.

—AGNIESZKA RADWAŃSKA

• • •

My tennis grunt isn't "Boogie Nights." It sounds like a ninety-year-old man, lifting a frozen turkey out of a Toyota Corolla.

——JASON GAY

• • •

I think tennis is a little dull. We need a little charisma, we need a little shouting, we need a little disagreement. You've got to have a little pizzazz.

——NICK BOLLETTIERI

• • •

I know I can rely well on my defense, but I also wouldn't like necessarily to stay in the back of the court for most of the match. I know that the matches against the top rivals at this level are won when you are aggressive and when you're taking the ball early. The first shot, serve, being aggressive and constructive in the right points, that's what I focus on.

—NOVAK DJOKOVIC

• • •

Tatiana from Moscow, Russia, via Wikimedia Commons

If it's not going to be a great match, make it quick.
—DOUGLAS ROBSON

• • •

Presuming that both players are healthy when taking the court, it comes down to the ability to dig deep and come up with the key shots in the critical moments to put an opponent away.
—JACK GALLAGHER

• • •

Every spring someone trots out the claim that the flurry of buzzer-beaters in the NCAA basketball tournament makes it the most riveting event in sports, and there's always the World Cup, but what's happening in tennis feels far more intimate, close up, personal.
—JASON GAY

• • •

Veronaa, courtesy of iStockphoto

The person driving the fancy little sports car may look like he (or she) should come in first. I'll put my money on the grease monkey in the modified stock car who knows how to get around the track. It's the same for tennis.

— BRAD GILBERT AND STEVE JAMISON,
Winning Ugly

• • •

You can't learn that in a book what Lindsay went through, what Billie Jean King went through, what I went through, what Chrissie Evert went through—winning these Grand Slams and being No. 1 and all that. Nobody can teach that.

— MARTINA NAVRATILOVA

• • •

When I was eleven years old, I decided I wanted to be the best tennis player in the world—and I committed myself to that goal.
—BILLIE JEAN KING

• • •

If you're a champion, you have to have it in your heart.
—CHRIS EVERT

• • •

Tennis was so much more than a game. What you saw—four people, a ball, and lines that determined whether a ball was in or out—was but an illusion.
—ABRAHAM VERGHESE,
The Tennis Partner

• • •

Tennis fans understand their sport has it all—love, power, sex,
money, violence, aggression, manipulation—the whole spectrum
of human behavior, even the occasional sporting gesture
or humane touch.

—GEORGE VECSEY,
Tennis and the Meaning of Life

• • •

I submit that tennis is the most beautiful sport there is and
also the most demanding. It requires body control, hand-eye
coordination, quickness, flat-out speed, endurance, and that
weird mix of caution and abandon we call courage.

—DAVID FOSTER WALLACE

• • •

Tennis is a sport based on very quick, explosive movement,
unlike, for example, a quarterback in football or
a pitcher in baseball.
—PATRICK MCENROE

• • •

In general playing against top players, you always put yourself in
a situation where you have got to push yourself. To be the
best you've got to beat the best.
—VICTORIA AZARENKA

• • •

I thought that when I won Wimbledon at seventeen, I thought
that would be the most treasured moment of my career. But
when I fell down on my knees today I realized that this was
extremely special, and even more so.
—MARIA SHARAPOVA (AFTER SHE WON HER CAREER GRAND SLAM)

• • •

Tennis gives kids a pathway to a better life through education.
It gives them a springboard for staying out of trouble, staying
fit and active and ultimately having a better life.
—OLGA HARVEY (SENIOR DIRECTOR OF COMMUNICATIONS
AND STRATEGIC PLANNING FOR NEW YORK JUNIOR
TENNIS & LEARNING [NYJTL])

• • •

PART THREE

Grand Slams

Pete Sampras was a traditionalist; to him, tennis was all about
the four Grand Slam events.

—PETER BODO

• • •

This is a sport I love truly with all my heart. Because I love the
sport, that's why I started playing it. As a kid you dream to be in
a position to win Grand Slams, win the season finale and be the
best in the world. I managed to achieve that for many times.

—NOVAK DJOKOVIC

• • •

Grand Slams

I had so many outs in my career. I could have said, I don't need this. I have money; I have fame; I have victories; I have Grand Slams. But when your love for something is bigger than all those things, you continue to keep getting up in the morning when it's freezing outside, when you know that it can be the most difficult day, when nothing is working, when you feel like the belief sometimes isn't there from the outside world, and you seem so small.

—MARIA SHARAPOVA

• • •

When you're five years old and you see Grand Slams on TV, you want to be part of it and you work for fifteen to twenty years to have the level to play those kind of tournaments.

——PIERRE HUGUES-HERBERT

• • •

There's a reason pundits tend not to pick "Top Grand Slam" in their annual awards. It just doesn't feel right to compare these four tournaments. Each one is an epic that produces multiple, enthralling storylines and worthy champions who earn the singles titles the hard way.

——PETER BODO

• • •

AUSTRALIAN OPEN

I would think the Australian Open is the one where players come in maybe most inspired. It's always been my most consistent Slam, maybe until last year. I have always played very well here.

—ROGER FEDERER

• • •

It felt pretty hot, like you're dancing in a frying pan.

—VICTORIA AZARENKA

• • •

I put the bottle down on the court and it started melting a little bit underneath, the plastic, so you knew it was warm.
—CAROLINE WOZNIACKI (2014)

• • •

Fourth time in seven years that the Women's Final at the Australian Open lasted fifteen or fewer games. Not a reliable ticket to buy.
—BEN ROTHENBERG

• • •

WIMBLEDON

I always say Wimbledon is a really unique experience. Lining up, being able to get tickets . . . it's a wonderful experience. I think it's pretty cool. It's like no other tournament.
—SERENA WILLIAMS

• • •

At that very moment, I knew what I wanted more than anything: I wanted to lift the Wimbledon Cup over my head, hear the crowd cheer, and know I had become the number one player in the world.
—NOVAK DJOKOVIC,
Serve to Win

• • •

I still remember the first time I walked into the grounds noticing the littlest things like the flowers, everything was so well manicured, so pretty . . . it was stunning. I always compare it to when I first went to Disneyland, you walk in and you say "Wow!" and I had the same feeling at Wimbledon.

—KIM CLIJSTERS

I read this princess magazine story. One story was about this girl who trained and was taken to this place called Wimbledon where she won on this magical court. I didn't know it was for real but she said "yes, this place exists in England."

—EVONNE GOOLAGONG

Julie Ganz

Whatever happened in my career or my tennis or mentally, it happened for a reason. In a lot of ways, I felt like I was born to win Wimbledon.

——PETE SAMPRAS

• • •

When I was eight or nine years old, I had two dreams. One to be part of the Swedish Davis Cup team and the second to play on Wimbledon Centre Court.

——BJÖRN BORG

• • •

Grand Slams

Since I was a kid, I was dazzled by Becker's performances at Wimbledon. This guy was such a character, he jumped around, he dived. . . . Since then, I've been dreaming of winning this tournament.

—DAVID NALBANDIAN

• • •

He *was* Wimbledon. As he accumulated trophies and tied Björn Borg's record of five consecutive titles, all the while fitting in so flawlessly, Federer came to overtake the event.

—L. JON WERTHEIM,
Strokes of Genius

• • •

Wimbledon has never been a place for timid tennis players, and no one who relied more on guile than athleticism has won this event since Martina Hingis in 1997.
—TOM PERROTTA

• • •

There's a little-known British ordinance stating that Wimbledon must generate at least a dozen breathless faux scandals per tournament.
—L. JON WERTHEIM

• • •

Grand Slams

When Novak Djokovic won Wimbledon for the first time,
I watched him yank out a bit of grass and eat it. Weird, but
I completely got where Djokovic was coming from.

—JASON GAY

• • •

Playing on grass returns you not just to the origins of the game,
whose official name after all is lawn tennis, but beyond that to
the primal, paradisal world of earliest childhood play where
there is no greater delight than to run and tumble
on the greensward.

—HARRY EYRES

• • •

They're tennis geeks, and now they've both got Wimbledon titles.
—JUDY MURRAY,
on sons Andy and Jamie

• • •

Wimbledon is like a drug. Once you win it, you've just got
to do it again.
—MARTINA NAVRATILOVA

• • •

I've had a love affair with Wimbledon for a long time.
—ANDY RODDICK

• • •

I told my coach Nick Bolletieri that I was never going back. It didn't leave the best imprint on my memory, but one of my great regrets was responding to that by not playing for a few years.

—ANDRE AGASSI,
on his first Wimbledon

• • •

You can't even wear off white or cream. I was like, "Man, if you wash your whites too many times, they will be illegal."

—BETHANIE MATTEK-SANDS (ON THE DRESS CODE)

• • •

FRENCH OPEN

We built Roland Garros for them [the "Four Musketeers"], they were the reason the stadium was built, so it shows that at that time they were huge stars. Maybe because they were the first French team to have success.

——PHILIPPE BOUIN

• • •

You can't fake it out here. I move horrendously out here. My first step is just so bad on this stuff. I feel like I'm always shuffling or hopping or not stopping or something. My footwork on this stuff is really bad.

——ANDY RODDICK

• • •

Grand Slams

A quick surface and skating footwork have proved [the French
Open] to be, for many, the most difficult jewel of
the bunch to collect.
—JONATHAN BASS

• • •

It's very strange, but here, it's magic here. It's a place where I feel
really good, and I can go beyond myself and play a type of tennis
I wouldn't even think of. Even today before the match, if people
told me, "You are going to play four hours with such a score,"
I wouldn't have believed it. So there is magic to some extent.
—GAËL MONFILS

• • •

[Federer's win at the 2009 French Open] definitely made us sit up
and realize that through persistence and continual trying,
we can conquer our demons.

——THADDEUS MCCARTHY

• • •

What won't you hear on these grounds? You won't hear a PA
announcer, in a shiny, slippery voice straight fresh from PA
announcer school, advise you to stay hydrated. You won't hear
him tell you, erroneously, that one of the show courts is filled and
that you should "enjoy the doubles action on the side courts,"
while not forgetting to stop by the food court and a
T-shirt vendor while you're at it.

——STEVE TIGNOR

• • •

US OPEN

Every Grand Slam has something unique about it. New York is about night session. You know, music, entertainment, crowd interaction. It's part of the show. It's part of what we do, and that's why this tournament is so special.

—NOVAK DJOKOVIC

• • •

Two sets to up . . . two sets to zero . . . I lost my words. I don't know what I'm talking anymore.

—MARIN ČILIĆ,
after a five-set match against Jo-Wilfried Tsonga

• • •

We wanted to be like Andre. You need that kind of champion to inspire more American kids to go out and pick up a racquet.
—BOB AND MIKE BRYAN

• • •

slgckgc, via Wikimedia Commons

I look forward to ending on my home turf at the US Open.
There's still a lot of fight left in me.
—ANDRE AGASSI,
on his retirement

• • •

I don't think I would take a vacation at Flushing Meadows.
—MARTINA NAVRATILOVA

• • •

PART FOUR

Davis Cup

We all know that the Davis Cup is a very special competition and playing in the Davis Cup final is the biggest success that my country ever had.

—NOVAK DJOKOVIC

• • •

I've always known, once I got a taste of playing Davis Cup, if I were given an opportunity to be the captain, I would certainly want to take it.

—JIM COURIER

• • •

Davis Cup

Obviously, the world has caught up to [the US] when it comes to
the highest level of tennis, and I think that's a great thing.
It's great for tennis. It's a global sport.

——PAT MCENROE

• • •

The strongest feelings I experienced were in Davis Cup. It was the
most powerful thing, the victories and the losses. It hits
you in a distinct way. It's another level of satisfaction;
another level of sadness.

——DAVID NALBANDIAN

• • •

Players feel the team camaraderie and the pride and
responsibility for their nation and need to manage that.
—JIM COURIER

• • •

In an era when most world-class tennis, including the Davis Cup,
Wimbledon, and the other major tournaments, was amateur,
and players played for glory, not money, the Davis Cup was
the most important trophy in tennis and one of the biggest
competitions in world sports.
—MARSHALL JON FISHER,
A Terrible Splendor

• • •

Davis Cup

AP Photo/Kevork Djansezian

I have sometimes played my best Davis Cup matches away from home when you stay in the moment a bit more. But it is tough when half the crowd are spitting on you.

—LLEYTON HEWITT

• • •

[Davis Cup's] the event that I felt was different from the others. The pressure, the support of the people. It's something unique.

—DAVID NALBANDIAN

• • •

Davis Cup

I regret maybe not celebrating as much as I should have done after some of my other wins, because now I know how much effort goes into achieving them. You never know when the next one might come—it may never—so we should make the most it.

—ANDY MURRAY

• • •

PART FIVE

More Reflections and Insight from the Pros

Tennis is a perfect combination of violent action taking place in an atmosphere of total tranquility.

—BILLIE JEAN KING

• • •

A lot of things changed for me in the seven years between
Slams, but not the indescribably joyful sensation of
hitting a tennis ball well.

—ROD LAVER,
The Education of a Tennis Player (with Bud Collins)

• • •

You live during the match, and you have strong emotions, but
you don't want to get too overexcited. My body's totally flat
now. I cannot move anymore. I'm totally exhausted, just
because of the tension out there.

—ROGER FEDERER

• • •

. . . Federer, in addition to all the winning, has been able to
conjure such ethereal tennis while matching the firepower of his
rivals and at a time when so many things—the rackets,
the strings, the courts, the size, strength and speed of the
players—conspire against the expression of beauty in tennis . . .

—MICHAEL STEINBERGER

• • •

In my own mind, I felt like, when Jimmy Connors was at his best,
I thought he was the best player who ever played. Then along
came Borg and Ivan Lendl, and . . . I wondered how in the world
anyone could play tennis better than that? Then there was Pete
Sampras. . . . It does just keep getting better.

—CLIFF DRYSDALE

• • •

Suyk, Koen/Anefo, via Wikimedia Commons

The good things come when you never expect it most of the
time. When you want something too much and say this
is the moment I have to do this and that, it's always
going to be a big mess.

—FLAVIA PENNETTA

• • •

I remember as a kid, I was improvising and making little trophies
out of different materials and going in front of the mirror, lifting
the trophies and saying "Nole was the champion!"

—NOVAK DJOKOVIC

• • •

In tennis, I could get noticed more: if I won it was all down to me, and if I lost it wasn't because ten other players had let me down. I could play the match my own way.
—ILIE NASTASE,
Mr. Nastase: The Autobiography

• • •

Sometimes it's almost better to lose against a guy outside of the top 50. It's not a guy you play all the time. Losing against fellow top-10 players sometimes can play tricks on your mind, and that's when the match-ups come into play.
—ROGER FEDERER

• • •

The finish line at the end of a career is no different from the finish line at the end of a match. The objective is to get within reach of that finish line, because then it gives off a magnetic force.

—ANDRE AGASSI,
Open

• • •

I will never ever in my life replace that first 30 seconds after winning a big match. That's gone. That's not coming back. That adrenaline rush doesn't exist for me anymore, although that's before fatherhood.

—ANDY RODDICK

• • •

When I was younger, I was a robot. Wind her up
and she plays tennis.

—CHRIS EVERT

• • •

My serve and my forehand I pretty much always had, but my
backhand was a made backhand. I worked on it for years.

—IVAN LENDL

• • •

When you do something best in life, you don't really want to
give that up—and for me it's tennis.

—ROGER FEDERER

• • •

Tennis players are athletes and shot-makers—but also
decision-makers.

—CARL BIALIK

• • •

I hate to lose more than I like to win. I hate to see the happiness
on their faces when they beat me!

—JIMMY CONNORS

• • •

For my whole career I have been motivated by losses. So that's
just been my thing. When I lose, I just get better.

—SERENA WILLIAMS

• • •

When a tennis player loses a match, he or she must face the pain all alone. There are no teammates to turn to, no caddy to give an enthusiastic pat on the back as the match slips from one's grasp.

—KEVIN CRAFT

• • •

I always wanted to help make tennis a team sport.

—BILLIE JEAN KING

• • •

When I stop playing, it's not going to be because I'm sick of playing . . . It's going to be because I'm sick of practicing.
—SERENA WILLIAMS

• • •

[Serena] knows that when push comes to shove she can uncork it or just play her 75 percent and it's harder than 100 percent of somebody else's.
—MARTINA NAVRATILOVA

• • •

Hard work is something you will find amongst everyone that is at the top of their field, their sport, their profession. It's something you can't take for granted and it is what gets you through those tough moments and really take you from being good, to being great, to being extraordinary.

——MILOS RAONIC

• • •

Every tournament for me is just a bonus at this point in my career. So it's an interesting place to be at.

——SERENA WILLIAMS

• • •

I think every person has a passion in life, and mine is for tennis.

——MONICA SELES

• • •

http://www.flickr.com/photos/madmarlin_/ via Wikimedia Commons

I'm playing well, I'm fit, and dammit if I'm not hungry!
——MILOS RAONIC

• • •

Every time I walk into this room, everyone expects me to win
every single match. As much as I would like to be a robot,
I'm not. I try to.
——SERENA WILLIAMS

• • •

What impresses me even more than the physical prowess of Serena is the fact that she can still conjure up that hunger and that passion for these matches. . . . Sometimes, (the motivation is) just not there. And the times when it wasn't there for her, she still created magic.

—CHRIS EVERT

• • •

I just love [Serena Williams] so much. I get goose bumps when I talk about it, but . . . her walk through the shadows of history? You know, she's the Jordan of all sports.

—ANDY RODDICK

• • •

More Reflections and Insight from the Pros

If you know anything about me, I hate to lose. I've always said I hate losing more than I like winning, so that drives me to be the best that I can be.

——SERENA WILLIAMS

• • •

Today probably this is my last cheeseburger, and then tomorrow pasta, real pasta at home.

——ROBERTA VINCI

• • •

Serena's 2015 should go down as the most relentlessly awesome year in women's tennis and one of the most remarkable years in the history of US sports.

——BILL BRADLEY

• • •

To be the best, year after year, takes a good team of support with coach and trainer. It's having to play through times when you aren't playing well and trying to find a way to win those matches you have to win.

——PETE SAMPRAS

• • •

Tennis player and coach are in a much more intimate relationship than, say, a halfback or left fielder is with his coach—plus in team sports the credit or blame is usually distributed among a slew of coaches.

—PETER BODO

• • •

One of the biggest dangers in a tennis match is getting mentally thrown off course by a series of poor points. One negative thought builds on another, and before long a player's whole mindset is so toxic that there is no way he can possibly play well, let alone win the match.

—FLORIO PANAIOTTI

• • •

I play each point like my life depends on it.
——RAFAEL NADAL

• • •

If I had to choose one man to play for my life, it would be Nadal.
——JIM COURIER

• • •

I never wanted to be the great guy or the colorful guy or the interesting guy. I wanted to be the guy who won matches.
—PETE SAMPRAS

• • •

In tennis, sometimes even the smallest thing can change the course of a match.
—JIMMY CONNORS,
The Outsider

• • •

I'm a perfectionist. I'm pretty much insatiable. I feel there's so many things I can improve on.
—SERENA WILLIAMS

• • •

From the beginning, I decided that if people came to me later on and told me my daughters were great tennis players, I had failed. Success would be if they came up to me and said my daughters were great people.

—RICHARD WILLIAMS,
Black and White: The Way I See It

• • •

The dumber you are on court, the better you're going to play.

—JIM COURIER

• • •

I don't believe in perfection, no? I really don't like to talk about
perfection, because that, my opinion, doesn't exist.
You can play always better.
—RAFAEL NADAL

• • •

Tennis is mostly mental. You win or lose the match before
you even go out there.
—VENUS WILLIAMS

• • •

I love the fact that tennis is such a mental game. The player with the strongest mental fortitude often wins in those situations when it's win by two games.
—ALICIA MOLIK

• • •

[Jennifer Capriati] was fun to watch because she was always happy and giggly and just killing everybody from the start.
—MARY JOE FERNANDEZ

• • •

What matters isn't how well you play when you're playing well. What matters is how well you play when you're playing badly.
—MARTINA NAVRATILOVA

• • •

Michal.Pohorelsky, www.Multimediaexpo.cz, via Wikimedia Commons

I'm not afraid of anyone, but sometimes I'm afraid of myself. The mental part is very important.
——JUSTINE HENIN

• • •

[The ATP Tour] is much more physical, much more mental. You just have to be mature in both areas to succeed at a high level. You just can't come out of the blue anymore.
——MARDY FISH

• • •

I've always said the next best thing to playing and winning is playing and losing, because at least I'm playing tennis.

—JIMMY CONNORS,
The Outsider

• • •

All night and this morning I thought about what I would do, how I would play, and if I would win or not. And then when I won the last point, I felt . . . I felt . . . I felt free.

—JO-WILFRIED TSONGA

• • •

I would like interviews to be more like in boxing . . . they bring
what their fans want: war, blood, emotion. All that is missing
in tennis, where everything is clean and white, with polite
handshakes and some nice shots.

——ERNESTS GULBIS

• • •

[Tennis] needs a little controversy. It needs a little Dennis
Rodman type of guy. It needs a little more hatred, or whatever
you want to call it.

——PETE SAMPRAS

• • •

Too many people asking too many questions in tennis.
Golf is better.

——IVAN LENDL

• • •

AP Photo/G. Paul Burnett

One reason why I love tennis so much is that it is the truest form of democracy in sports. If you win, you rise in the rankings and make money. If you lose, you either ask your parents for more money—if you have rich parents—look for a sponsor, or quit playing and find another job.

—VINCE SPADEA (AND DAN MARKOWITZ),
Break Point

• • •

I welcome the added pressure of being alone on the court because that pressure is what makes tennis one of the best sports in the world.

—SLOANE STEPHENS

• • •

I love the winning. I can take the losing, but most of all I love to play.

—BORIS BECKER

• • •

If they had rankings in baseball, maybe I would have been able to do the math and figure out my chances of being a professional baseball player versus a tennis player. But that was the decision-maker for me, I just thought I was better in tennis.

—JIM COURIER

• • •

[My dad] was convinced if my eyes were going to move around as a little baby, I might as well be looking at a tennis ball.

—ANDRE AGASSI

• • •

I defy you to find a top-ten player who *wasn't* driven, at first
anyway, by at least one of his parents.

—DOMINIC COBELLO WITH MIKE AGASSI,
The Agassi Story

• • •

What a polite game tennis is. The chief word in it seems to be
"sorry" and admiration of each other's play crosses the net as
frequently as the ball.

—JAMES MATTHEW BARRIE

• • •

Tennis is, more than most sports, a sport of the mind; it is the player who has those good sensations on the most days, who manages to isolate himself best from his fears and from the ups and downs in morale a match inevitably brings, who ends up being world number one.

—RAFAEL NADAL,
Rafa

• • •

When you step out on the court, I don't think anybody thinks about age. Because if you're out on this tour, it means you deserve to be here. You've got the skill. It must mean you know how to play.

—VENUS WILLIAMS

• • •

Venus and Serena were taught that they were the best, and they
[still] believe that they are.
——RICHARD WILLIAMS

• • •

It just so happens that I love to play, I love to compete. I'm
having fun. I just really can't let it go. . . . I don't want to let go.
I won't let go.
——SERENA WILLIAMS

• • •

AP Photo/David Vincent

I was so flabbergasted at the amount of money paid out to professional players that Mrs. Williams and I thought the best thing we could do for our children is to give them the ability to play tennis.

—RICHARD WILLIAMS

• • •

The fifth set is not about tennis, it's about nerves.

—BORIS BECKER

• • •

I like the individuality of tennis. You have to rely on yourself,
and that makes things interesting.

—ANDY RODDICK

• • •

The tennis match doesn't care how tall you are, how short
you are. This is the game.

—LI NA

• • •

Tennis is the only sport I know of where you have your locker right next to your opponent. You see him naked. You see him go to the bathroom. You see him take a shower. Imagine doing that in boxing. Or in basketball. Or in football. Then, you go out and play for fame and glory and money.

—BORIS BECKER

• • •

When we get on the court and the crowd cheers your name or salutes you—it's like you're a gladiator in the arena. And everyone is cheering—and you're fighting, you're screaming, during your strokes—it feels like you're an animal, fighting for your life.

—NOVAK DJOKOVIC

• • •

Being a champion was not a job, it was the life [Djokovic]
had chosen.
—SIMON BARNES

• • •

I played with the same racquet for like four months. Just let the
strings get less and less tension—what did I care?
—PAM SHRIVER

• • •

Legendary? I don't know. I'm just Serena.
——SERENA WILLIAMS

• • •

I'm just about winning.
——SERENA WILLIAMS

• • •

Right now I'm the first guy at 999.
—DANIEL NESTOR,
on the anticipation of winning 1,000 doubles
matches on the ATP World Tour

• • •

It's always the same after winning a big title. You are
a little bit lost in your mind.
—STAN WAWRINKA

• • •

Tennis was never work for me, tennis was fun. And the tougher
the battle and the longer the match, the more fun I had.

——JIMMY CONNORS

• • •

It's a tossup as to which is quicker, [Andy] Roddick's rocket serve
or his rapier wit.

——KAREN CROUSE

• • •

I play Cinderella tennis . . . I can't quite get to the ball.
—LARRY ADLER

• • •

Tennis fans watch Roger and Rafa and Serena and Novak not just for their dazzling shot-making and athleticism. We watch because we want to relate to, take something from, and join in their struggles and triumphs.
—STEVE TIGNOR

• • •

The day before Venus and Serena arrived, the game was a fully functioning system complete with plots and subplots and rivalries. The day after Venus and Serena arrived, all that seemed about as relevant as political squabbles in Constantinople right after the Turks showed up.

—BRIAN PHILLIPS

• • •

I made it look so easy on court all those years. No one realized how hard I had to work. No one realized how much I had to put into it. They underestimated my intensity.

—PETE SAMPRAS

• • •

When I was forty, my doctor advised me that a man in his forties shouldn't play tennis. I heeded his advice carefully and could hardly wait until I reached fifty to start again.

——HUGO BLACK

• • •

Katharine Hepburn said at Humphrey Bogart's funeral that he liked to drink, so he drank; Serena likes to win tennis matches, so she wins tennis matches.

——BRIAN PHILLIPS

• • •

[Serena] leaps into the air, she laughs, she grins, she pumps her fist, she points her index finger to the sky, signaling she's No. 1. Her joy is palpable.

——CLAUDIA RANKINE

• • •

"Good shot," "bad luck," and "Hell" are the five basic words to be used in tennis.

——VIRGINIA GRAHAM,
Say Please

• • •

A person's tennis game begins with his nature and background
and comes out through his motor mechanisms into shot
patterns and characteristics of play.

—JOHN MCPHEE,
Levels of the Game

• • •

To be a tennis champion, you have to be inflexible.
You have to be stubborn. You have to be arrogant.
You have to be selfish and self-absorbed.

—CHRIS EVERT

• • •

You can lead a tennis player to clay, but you can't make him rally.

—PETER BODO,

The Clay Ran Red

• • •

The depressing thing about tennis is that no matter how good
I get, I'll never be as good as a wall.

—MITCH HEDBERG

• • •

Tennis and golf are best played, not watched.
—ROGER KAHN

• • •

I discovered there was a lot of work to being good in tennis.
You've got to make a lot of sacrifices and spend a lot of time
if you really want to achieve with this sport, or in any sport,
or in anything truly worthwhile.
—ARTHUR ASHE

• • •

Lleyton Hewitt. His two greatest strengths are his legs, his speed,
his agility, and his competitiveness.

—PAT CASH

• • •

I'm not a very good morning person. I'm No. 1 in the world,
so I should have the right, if I'm going to play on center court,
to say what time I want to play.

—MARTINA HINGIS

• • •

The trouble with me is that every match I play against five
opponents: umpire, crowd, ball boys, court, and myself.

—GORAN IVANIŠEVIĆ

• • •

If I could, I'd give my win to Serena at the US Open.
Unfortunately, it doesn't work that way.
—VENUS WILLIAMS,
after the Serena Slam came to an end

• • •

What more can you say that hasn't already been said about
Venus Williams? She is the personification of class
and grace as a competitor.
—KATRINA ADAMS (USTA CHARIMAN, CEO, AND PRESIDENT)

• • •

Eurosport, via Wikimedia Commons

Tennis helped give me an identity and made me feel
like somebody.

—CHRIS EVERT

• • •

It's very difficult for a regular guy to go hit a 150 m.p.h. serve
without having his shoulder end up in St. Louis.

—JIMMY CONNORS

• • •

Does any shot in tennis command more respect and resonate
with a greater sense of authority and finality than
the service ace?

—PETER BODO

• • •

I was always comfortable hitting an overhead, even as a kid.
It was like an easier serve.
—PETE SAMPRAS

• • •

Just looking at my career doesn't happen very often. And I think
[it's because] I had such peace of mind that I felt I gave my sport
everything. . . . I think the comfort was that I felt like I gave
everything to it and it gave me a lot in return.
—STEFFI GRAF

• • •

[Steffi Graf] played like a robot, like a machine, no emotions . . .
strong with a stone face.
—CLAUDIA KOHDE-KILSCH

• • •

Chris Eason, via Wikimedia Commons

[Graf] was winning her matches so fast. People went out against Steffi knowing they were going to lose, it was a just a matter of how long you were able to keep her out there.

——MARY JOE FERNANDEZ

• • •

It is not good for [Pete] Sampras to get too close to [Andre] Agassi, on court or off, since what makes their rivalry work is their contrasts, not their similarities.

——BERNIE LINCICOME

• • •

What rivalry? I win all the matches.
——MARTINA HINGIS

• • •

All I could ever see was my opponent—you could set off
dynamite on the next court and I wouldn't notice.
——MAUREEN CONNOLLY

• • •

The tennis circuit is often characterized as a
"traveling road show." But it also takes on the
dimensions of a close-knit community.
—L. JON WERTHEIM,
Strokes of Genius

• • •

I think if you love the game and you enjoy it, there's no end.
You don't have to just say that's it.
—ROD LAVER

• • •

The main thing is he still enjoys the game and is
a student of the game.

—ROD LAVER,
on Roger Federer

• • •

It would be kind of like when somebody dies [if Federer retires].
I know, because I had that feeling when Björn Borg suddenly
retired [in 1981]. He was so much bigger than the
game, it seemed.

—CHRIS EVERT

• • •

If my career just lets people know you have to do it your own
way, because I have been criticized plenty for the style of play,
keeping a coach too long, [etc.]. And I knew what I was doing
was the right way and was the best way for me to have success.

—JAMES BLAKE

• • •

Athletes have a certain stubbornness that carries us through and makes us do things that people say we can't do.

—KIM CLIJSTERS

• • •

Everyone wins in tennis because everyone starts with love.

—SALLY HUSS,
Eight Golden Rules for How to Play Your Best Tennis

• • •

You don't have to hate your opponents to beat them.
—KIM CLIJSTERS

• • •

I had a goal. I wanted to beat my mom first. And my parents and my brother. And that was the ultimate goal.
—CAROLINE WOZNIACKI

• • •

The champion [Federer] quickly turned himself into an exemplary ambassador for the sport; it's not a coincidence that the champions who followed him, Rafael Nadal and Novak Djokovic, have done the same.

—STEVE TIGNOR

• • •

I had the good luck and the bad luck to coincide with practically the two best players in the history of world tennis. . . . To have shared this great era with [Federer and Nadal], to have beaten them, lost to them and been at this level has given me a lot of pride.

—DAVID NALBANDIAN

• • •

Luck has nothing to do with it, because I have spent many, many hours, countless hours, on the court working for my one moment in time, not knowing when it would come.

—SERENA WILLIAMS

• • •

To be the one that everybody wants to take away the position of the title of being the best tennis player in the world is obviously a lot of responsibility and it also demands a lot of professionalism and devotion to what you do.

—NOVAK DJOKOVIC

• • •

This was like a lion being in a cage, and now you're going to let this lion out and she gets to perform. I couldn't believe how [Venus] was hitting the ball.
—RICK MACCI,
on Venus Williams's pro debut in 1994

• • •

In tennis the addict moves about a hard rectangle and seeks to ambush a fuzzy ball with a modified snow-shoe.
—ELLIOTT CHAZE

• • •

Somebody once told me that tennis is your husband, your boyfriend, your fiancé, and your best friend all rolled into one. . . . It had also been my adolescence, my education, my entry into adulthood, and my ticket to see the world.

—MONICA SELES,
Getting a Grip

• • •

Some of our sports teams and Olympians have done extremely well, like the rowers and cyclists, but for someone to perform like Andy [Murray] week in and week out in an individual sport which is so global, so accessible—I can't think of anyone who competes with that.

—ROSS HUTCHINS

• • •

AP Photo/John Rooney

Speed in tennis is a strange mixture of intuition, guesswork,
footwork and hair-trigger reflexes.

—EUGENE SCOTT

• • •

In normal matches, maybe a quarterfinal match or first-round match, I don't get so worked up so much anymore, where I have knots in my tummy. But I do still get nervous, I still care very dearly and still have the fire. I think that will never go away until the day is there where I retire and everything drops away.

——ROGER FEDERER

• • •

The first time I won a tournament, the first time I won a Grand Slam, the first time I won the Davis Cup—those are moments you'll never forget. And then of course, the moment I said good-bye to the game was a pretty indelibly seared into my memory.

——ANDRE AGASSI

• • •

I don't see myself without tennis. It's something I did since
I was young, so I don't know what else I can do.
I don't know what I like.
——FLAVIA PENNETTA

• • •

We're asking the tennis players to play three weeks on and a week
off or two weeks on. And if they're a good player of LeBron's
caliber, within our tournaments, that means they will play 15
nights out of 21, playing 2½ hours a night, at the highest level,
without any substitutions. Think of the effect on the athlete's
body every day without any substitutes.
——WOMEN'S TENNIS ASSOCIATION CEO STEVE SIMON

• • •

I always play my best tennis when I play for my country.
—ANDY MURRAY

• • •

Even though it's never fun being on the not-winning side,
it's better than not playing at all.
—ROGER FEDERER

• • •

I've got some good news and bad news. The good news is
I dreamed about tennis last night. The bad news is
everybody better watch out.
—SERENA WILLIAMS

• • •

I think tennis is the greatest sport in the world. Because, first of all, it's based on merit on the court. It's a combination of physical, mental, technical and tactical skills. It's one on one. It's international. And it's just a great feeling hitting that ball cleanly and purely.

—JUSTIN GIMELSTOB

• • •

Understand that you are part of something that is greater than you. Tennis is greater than all of us.

—NOVAK DJOKOVIC

• • •

Tennis is designed to focus on nationalism. . . . In tennis, the only "team" you represent is your home country.
—BOB AND MIKE BRYAN

• • •

annie, via Wikimedia Commons

I miss feeling so nervous that I would throw up before the finals of Wimbledon.
—PETE SAMPRAS

• • •

I am No. 8 in the world. I am not No. 100. It seems like I am No. 200 in every press conference. I am not so bad.
—RAFAEL NADAL

• • •

I'd as soon write free verse as play tennis with the net down.
—ROBERT FROST

• • •

PART SIX

Apparel

I suppose you could say that if it had been a really nice animal, something sympathetic, then maybe nothing would have happened. Suppose I had picked a rooster. Well, that's French, but it doesn't have the same impact.

—RENÉ LACOSTE

• • •

I don't know why we put up with long flannel trousers for so long.

—BUNNY AUSTIN

• • •

Apparel

With his white linen hat and his flannel shorts, the little English player [Bunny Austin] looked like an A. A. Milne production.

—JOHN KIERAN

• • •

HultonArchive, courtesy of iStockphoto

196

Apparel

[Suzanne Lenglen] was scandalous in many different ways; sometimes sipping brandy in the changeovers. Suzanne really was a tennis icon who had a lot of influence on general fashion. Even the head wraps she'd wear to keep the hair out of her eyes became a fixture of 1920s fashion for women around Europe and the US.

—BEN ROTHENBERG

• • •

Gussie [Moran] wasn't a revolutionary. She wore the dress for two reasons. She wanted to look good, and the shorter dresses allowed her to move more freely on the court.

—TEDDY TINLING

• • •

Tennis is a sport where players value personal appearance and strive to take the court looking impeccable and exuding style.
——KEVIN CRAFT

• • •

I've been on tour for a long time. I've been wearing so many different designs. I just wanted to push the envelope again, just bring pop culture to tennis, kind of make it really fun.
——SERENA WILLIAMS

• • •

PART SEVEN

Doubles

Right when the match finished it was a relief. So much emotions.
I don't think we have ever done this kind of Dirty Dancing
swan dive. That was a first.

—MIKE BRYAN,
on winning 100th match with doubles partner and brother Bob

• • •

Not only will they go down in the record books as one of the greatest doubles pairings of all time, they will also be remembered for promoting and championing the game of doubles every step of the way.

—CHRIS KERMODE

• • •

[Doubles] is a subtle game of grace, ball placement, and movement, whose masters often make others feel foolish or simply tempt them to beat themselves.

—PAT BLASKOWER,
The Art of Doubles

• • •

Doubles

Doubles will never become an attritional test of power and endurance. It is a game of subtlety, of touch, of deft hands at the net.

— SIMON BRIGGS

• • •

You can almost watch a couple play mixed doubles and know whether they should stay together.

—DR. HERBERT HENDIN

• • •

[Roy] Emerson was the best doubles player of all the moderns, very possibly the best forehand player of all time. He was so quick he could cover everything. He had the perfect doubles shots, a backhand that dipped over the net and came in at the server's feet as he moved to net.

—JACK KRAMER

• • •

High-ranked singles players probably don't take [mixed doubles] so seriously, but actually that can make you play better, because you are more relaxed.

—ANA IVANOVIC

• • •

Doubles

In any partnership, there's got to be one person who brings the energy to the team, who takes all the pressure on their shoulder and drives the team forward. I know if I can keep Martina happy and relaxed, I don't even have to worry about the tennis.

—LEANDER PAES

• • •

An otherwise happily married couple may turn a mixed doubles game into a scene from *Who's Afraid of Virginia Woolf?*

—ROD LAVER

• • •

I don't think the combination of two older guys, nowadays especially, really makes sense any more. . . . The game's more athletic than it's ever been.

——DANIEL NESTOR

• • •

Unlike the players of [John] McEnroe's generation, contemporary stars play relatively little doubles, neglecting a prime opportunity to polish their net skills.

——PATRICK HRUBY

• • •

As long as it goes well, and I'm happy and healthy playing, I'd rather win the championships in doubles than playing one or two matches in the singles. Because physically, I couldn't cope with it anymore. So that's why I'd rather practice as much as I can and be competitive in the doubles.

——MARTINA HINGIS

• • •

PART EIGHT

A Shout-out to Table Tennis (Also Known as Ping-Pong)

It's a game without glamour. You feel you're doing something worthy and intelligent, but you know it's funny at the same time.
—HOWARD JACOBSON

• • •

Ping-Pong is everything.
—NANCY FRANKLIN

• • •

technotr, courtesy of iStockphoto

A Shout-out to Table Tennis (Also Known as Ping-Pong)

If you can't take a punch, you should play table tennis.
——PIERRE BERBIZIER

• • •

I'm good . . . but [Keanu Reeves] kicks my ass.
——PETER STORMARE

• • •

It's its own culture. We traveled all over the world together,
and he had table tennis friends everywhere.
——MARY DETSCH,
wife of the late table tennis great, Dick Miles

• • •

REFERENCES

WEBSITES

abc.net.au
ABC News
arthurashe.org
The Atlantic
ATP Tour
ausopen.com
The Australian
BBC.co.uk
biography.com
Bleacher Report
cnn.com
dailymail.co.uk
ESPN.com
Esquire
experiencelife.com
FanSided
foxnews.com
Fox Sports
The Globe and Mail
The Guardian
Huffington Post
Independent.co.uk
International Tennis Hall of Fame
insidetennis.com
Los Angeles Times

Men's Health
thenational.ae
News.com.au
New York Magazine
New York Times
Parade
The Players' Tribune
Sporting News
Sports Illustrated
St. Louis Post-Dispatch
Telegraph.co.uk
Tennis.com
Tennisnow.com
tennis-prose.com
tennispsychology.coms
Tennisworldusa.org
timesunion.com
Toronto Sun
US Magazine
US Open
USA Today
Vogue
Wall Street Journal
Wimbledon
WTA Tennis

BOOKS

Agassi, Andre. *Open*. Knopf, 2009.

Ashe, Arthur with Arnold Rampersad. *Days of Grace*. Knopf, 1993.

Blaskower, Pat. *The Art of Doubles*. Betray Books, 2007.

Bodo, Peter. *The Clay Ran Red*. Diversion Books, 2013.

Bodo, Peter. *The Courts of Babylon*. Scribner, 1995.

Bollettieri, Nick. *Bollettieri: Changing the Game*. New Chapter Publisher, 2014.

Cobello, Dominic with Mike Agassi. *The Agassi Story*. ECW Press, 2004.

Connors, Jimmy. *The Outsider*. Harper, 2013.

Court, Margaret. *Court on Court*. W.H. Allen/Virgin Books, 1976.

Cronin, Matthew. *Epic*. John Wiley & Sons, 2011.

Deford, Frank. *Big Bill Tilden*. Simon and Schuster, 1976.

Djokovic, Novak. *Serve to Win*. Zinc Inc., 2013.

Flink, Steve. *The Greatest Tennis Matches of All Time*. New Chapter Press, 2012.

Fox, Allen. *Think to Win*. Harper Perennial, 1993.

Gallwey, W. Timothy. *The Inner Game of Tennis*. Random House, 1974.

Gilbert, Brad and Steve Jamison. *Winning Ugly*. Touchstone, 1994.

Graham, Virginia. *Say Please*. The Harvill Press, 1949.

Huss, Sally. *Eight Golden Rules for How to Play Your Best Tennis*. Sally Huss Incorporated, 2012.

Jennings, Jay, ed. *Tennis and the Meaning of Life*. Mariner Books, 1996.

King, Billie Jean. *Pressure Is a Privilege*. LifeTime Media Inc., 2008.

Laver, Rod with Bud Collins. *The Education of a Tennis Player*. Simon & Schuster, 1971.

McEnroe, John. *Serious*. Little, Brown & Company, 2002.

McPhee, John. *Levels of the Game*. Farrar, Straus and Giroux, 1969.

Moran, Greg. *Tennis Beyond Big Shots*. Mansion Grove House, 2008.

Nadal, Rafael. *Rafa*. Hachette Books, 2011.

Nastase, Ilie. *Mr. Nastase: The Autobiography*. HarperCollins UK, 2004.

Perry, Fred. *Fred Perry, An Autobiography.* Arrow Books, 1985.

Seles, Monica. *Getting a Grip.* Avery, 2009.

Spadea, Vince and Dan Markowitz. *Break Point.* Sports Publishing, 2008.

USTA. *The Open Book.* Triumph Books, 2008.

Verghese, Abraham. *The Tennis Partner.* Harper, 1998.

Weir, Alison. *Henry VIII: The King and His Court.* Ballantine Books, 2008.

Wertheim, L. John. *Strokes of Genius.* Houghton Mifflin Harcourt, 2009.

Whitman, Malcolm D. *Tennis: Origins and Mysteries.* Dover Publications, 2004.

Williams, Richard. *Black and White*: *The Way I See It.* Atria Books, 2014.

INDEX

A

Adams, Franklin, 16
Adams, Katrina, 170
Adler, Larry, 162
Agassi, Andre, 26, 45, 56, 107, 113, 125, 150, 176, 188
Agassi, Mike, 151
Aggas, Luke, 33
Ashe, Arthur, 6, 8, 10, 21, 24, 168
Austin, Bunny, 194, 195
Australian Open, 97, 98
Azarenka, Victoria, 38, 77, 92, 97

B

backhand, ix, 56, 57, 78, 80, 126, 202
Bacsinszky, Timea, 41
Barnes, Simon, 158
Barrie, James Matthew, 151
Barzun, Jacques, 15
Bass, Jonathan, 109
Becker, Boris, 103, 149, 155, 167
Berdych, Tomas, 50
Bialik, Carl, 127
Black, Hugo, 164
Blake, James, 180
Bodo, Peter, 5, 94, 96, 137, 167, 172
Bollettieri, Nick, 10, 57, 60, 81, 85
Borg, Björn, 18, 19, 21, 28, 102, 103, 122, 180
Bouchard, Eugenie, 55

Bouin, Philippe, 108
Bradley, Bill, 136
Briggs, Simon, 201
Brown Grimes, Jane, 27
Bryan, Bob, 112, 192
Bryan, Mike, 59, 112, 192, 199

C

Cahill, Darren, 56
Canning Todd, Patricia, 13
Cash, Pat, 169
Chase, Chris, 29, 50
Chawkins, Steve, 24
Chaze, Elliott, 185
Čilić, Marin, 111
Clark, Anna, 61
Clijsters, Kim, 47, 100, 181, 182
Cobb, Ron, 2
Cobello, Dominic, 151
Cochet, Henri, 17, 76
Collins, Bud, 4, 16, 121
Connolly, Mauren, 177
Connors, Jimmy, 52, 122, 128, 139, 145, 161, 172
Courier, Jim, 114, 116, 138, 140, 150
Cowan, Barry, 67
Craft, Kevin, 36, 129, 198
Cronin, Matthew, 19
Crouse, Karen, 161

D
Deford, Frank, 22
Djokovic, Novak, 61, 67, 68, 86,
    94, 99, 105, 111, 114, 123, 157,
    158, 183, 184, 191
Drucker, Joel, 25
Drysdale, Cliff, 122

E
Elizabeth, Shannon, 81
Emerson, Roy, 78, 202
Evert, Chris, 89, 90, 126, 134, 166,
    171, 180
Eyres, Harry, 105

F
Federer, Roger, ix, 35, 42, 64, 69,
    97, 103, 110, 121, 124, 127, 179,
    180, 183, 188, 190
Fernandez, Mary Joe, 142, 176
Fish, Mardy, 144
Fisher, Marshall Jon, 116
Fleming, Peter, 59
forehand, ix, 23, 71, 80, 81, 126, 202
Foster Wallace, David, 91
Fox, Allen, 37
French Open, 108, 109, 110
Frost, Robert, 193

G
Gallagher, Jack, 87
Gallwey, W. Timothy, 78
Gay, Jason, 77, 85, 87, 105

Gibson, Althea, 17
Gilbert, Brad, 89
Gimelstob, Justin, 191
Godfrey, Honor, 3
Goolagong, Evonne, 9, 100
Graf, Steffi, 173, 174, 176
Graham, Virginia, 165
Greenberg, Mike, 32
Gulbis, Ernests, 146

H
Hart, Doris, 49
Hedberg, Mitch, 167
Hendin, Dr. Herbert, 201
Henin, Justine, 144
Henry VIII, 3
Hewitt, Lleyton, 44, 54, 55, 56, 66,
    118, 169
Hingis, Martina, 46, 104, 169, 177, 204
Hruby, Patrick, 55, 204
Hugues-Herbert, Pierre, 96
Huss, Sally, 181
Hutchins, Ross, 186

I
Iooss, Walter, 28
Isner, John, 47
Ivanišević, Goran, 169
Ivanovic, Ana, 202

J
Jamison, Steve, 89
Jones, Lolo, 29

INDEX

K

Kahn, Roger, 168
Kerber, Angelique, 75
Kermode, Chris, 200
Kieran, John, 195
King, Billie Jean, ix, 10, 11, 13, 89, 90, 120, 129
Kohde-Kilsch, Claudia, 174
Konta, Johanna, 63
Kramer, Jack, 202
Kudrow, Lisa, 51

L

Lacoste, Rene, 76, 194
Laver, Rod, 22, 23, 28, 62, 121, 178, 179, 203
Lendl, Ivan, 42, 45, 62, 122, 126, 146
Lenglen, Suzanne, 197
Lincicome, Bernie, 176

M

Macci, Rick, 185
Marble, Alice, 17
Mattek-Sands, Bethanie, 107
McCarthy, Thaddeus, 110
McEnroe, John, ix, 18, 19, 28, 47, 66, 204
McEnroe, Pat, 92, 115
McPhee, John, 166
Molik, Alicia, 142
Monfils, Gael, 109
Moran, Greg, 82
Moran, Gussie, 197

Mouratoglou, Patrick, 39
Murray, Andy, 15, 33, 49, 55, 72, 106, 119, 186, 190
Murray, Jim, 8, 9
Murray, Judy, 106

N

Na, Li, 156
Nadal, Rafael, 64, 73, 80, 138, 141, 152, 183, 193
Nadal, Toni, 75
Nalbandian, David, 103, 115, 118, 183
Nastase, Ilie, 124
Navratilova, Martina, 25, 38, 48, 72, 89, 106, 113, 130, 142
Nestor, Daniel, 160, 204
Nishikori, Kei, 83
Norman, Magnus, 57

P

Paes, Leander, 203
Panaiotti, Florio, 137
Pennetta, Flavia, 123, 189
Perrotta, Tom, 68, 104
Perry, Fred, 14, 15
Perry, Matthew, 51
Phillips, Brian, 163, 164
Price, S. L., 44, 71
Purcell, Mel, 62

R

Radwańska, Agnieszka, 84
Rankine, Claudia, 165

Raonic, Milos, 131, 133
Redford, Robert, 35
Robson, Douglas, 76, 87
Roddick, Andy, 30, 106, 108, 125, 134, 156, 161
Rosewall, Ken, 56
Rothenberg, Ben, 98, 107
Rusedski, Greg, 15

S
Sampras, Pete, 44, 52, 56, 71, 94, 102, 122, 136, 139, 146, 163, 173, 176, 193
Scott, Eugene, 187
Seles, Monica, ix, 24, 131, 186
serve, ix, 33, 35, 47, 59, 71, 83, 86, 126, 161, 172, 173, 179
Sharapova, Maria, 69, 80, 84, 93, 95
Shriver, Pam, 24, 158
Simon, Steve, 189
Smith, Stan, 18, 59
Spadea, Vince, 148
Steinberger, Michael, 121
Stephens, Sloane, 149
Stonebrook, Ian, 26

T
Taylor, David, 54
Tignor, Steve, 4, 18, 23, 110, 162, 183

Tilden, Bill, 16, 17, 22
Tinling, Teddy, 197
Tsonga, Jo-Wilfried, 111, 145

U
US Open, 8, 111, 113, 170

V
Vecsey, George, 91
Vinci, Roberta, 32, 135
volley, ix, 35, 59, 62

W
Watt, Lemeau, 22
Wawrinka, Stan, 36, 57, 160
Weir, Alison, 3
Wertheim, L. Jon, 103, 104, 178
Whitman, Malcolm D., 1
Wiedeman, Reeves, 27
Williams, Richard, 140, 153, 155
Williams, Serena, ix, 32, 41, 63, 83, 99, 128, 130, 131, 133, 134, 135, 139, 153, 159, 184, 190, 198
Williams, Venus, 39, 41, 141, 152, 153, 170, 185
Wimbledon, x, 93, 99, 100, 102, 103, 104, 105, 106, 107, 116, 193
Wolf, David, 8
Wozniacki, Caroline, 98, 182